Lapis Moon

Lapis Moon

Poems by

Christopher Brooks

Cover Art: Claudia Ribeiro
Author Photo: Vernon Hatley Photography
Cover design by Shay Culligan

ISBN: 978-1-952326-85-1

Kelsay Books
502 South 1040 East, A-119
American Fork, Utah, 84003

for Natachee

Acknowledgments

Many thanks to the people of Afghanistan. Like the Native Americans of my country, it's a miracle you've survived with your beautiful spirit intact, after lifetimes of suffering. Working amongst you was a highpoint in my life.

Special thanks to my wife Jen, mother-goddess. I feel most among the living when allowed to be a little crazy. Thanks for tolerating, sometimes encouraging, this. And to my daughter Tansy, piano heart, saxophone spirit. Even though you are only fifteen, I've learned a lifetime from you.

I'm grateful to the following publications in which some of the poems first appeared:

Hiram Poetry Review: "Slow Burn," "What We Used to Know"
Dragon Poet Review: "The Fighting Season," "Blue Democracy"
Blue Lake Review: "The Barber"
Deep South Magazine: "T-Bird"
Blue Collar Review: "Chicken Factory"
Fly Fishing and Tying Journal: "Just Fishing," "Oso Grill," "Lapis Moon"

Also by Christopher Brooks:
With Them I Move (Finishing Line Press, 2018)

A note on the use of "How Alike Are the Birds in The Olive Tree" by Sharon Jones. Permission was not obtained due to the death of its author. However, the poem was a personal gift, and I'm certain she would have approved of its use herein.

Table of Contents

All I want to know is what they call sin. Me, I have
never sinned unless you call it being alive.

—Linda Hogan

Ghost

It is time we find our spirit animals
For we know they guide us
Making sacred the earth

I am often afraid
I am no bear or wolf

I thought I was a dove
Always watching
But I can't stay put
Like the whirling stars
Like a crow at a cantina
Becoming an old man
A ghost
With black pointy boots
Singing songs in human language
Then vanishing

I must be a crow
For I have been a ghost all my life

The Fighting Season

for Natachee

Black locust, apple, apricot leaves
Another Afghan spring
The hollyhocks are low
Wrapped in deep green
When the time is right
The doves will pull their bow
Watching them grow
Tall as me

Jirga Center, remembering place
Inside your walls of peace
War roses pruned
For buds then blooms
Of red the fire of my mind
Of her lips
Missing
Having someone to miss

On the ground where the roses grow
A fissure in the fault
That coaxed these mountains to the sky
Through the heart of the earth my sprit goes
To watch her closing shop
Tired wonderful walk
Rose Woman

Birds migrated
Singing the long journey blues
Behind wrought iron spires disguised as flowers
Singing louder
To drown the diesel belch
And afterburners
Just outside

O mynah bird you are still here
Under the mulberry tree
But now delicate grass
Cushions your broken wing
I'm so glad you survived the winter
Even though the sky is your home

Desert morning
The muezzin's prayer
Drifts on a musical wind
Haunting and heavy
The weight of the West's fear

Beneath a pergola roof the sun on my face
Soon there will be shade
When the grapevine overhead
Throws out its leaves
But now its vines a brittle bark
No dew, no rain on this high Panjshir Plain
But the cut end of a vine
Drops something on my head cold and wet
That's how I know
The leaves will soon grow

Just outside these walls of peace
Rat-a-tat-tat
A suicide vest
The boys gone home to rest
But will never really leave
Their bones in the bark of a pomegranate tree

It is after the time when time stood still
Alexander the Great and the Soviets
Ahmed Shah Masood
Now time marches on
And with each new spring
With the pink and the red
The yellow and green
The fighting season

What We Used to Know

for Afghanistan

Behind concrete and barbed wire a laughing
dove shit on my notebook. An obvious sign.

I heard they tied a tiny bomb to one once but it
refused to fly over the target. Out of character

perhaps. They should call it what we do,
condemn it to mourning this borderline country.

We've learned nothing since climbing down
from trees. Clocks and smartphones were bad

enough. The day birds become an air force is the
day to boil down the bones of our humanity. Tear

down the schools. Plant trees in the rubble and
watch them grow tall. Hire birds to be our teachers

for free. Climb back into green canopies
where they'll teach us what we used to know.

T-Bird

for Tansy

Driving dirt section road.
Milk of moon dancing on the hood.
Pallid beams capitulating the night.
She said she realized the consequences of solitude
while passing Lady Liberty
on the Staten Island Ferry.
How she needed it too.
How poetry came to her for the first time that night.
How New York showed her
that she was just like me.

Lapis Moon

for Henry

On a high place over the walls I see
A village captured by night
Except when the moon is high
Above the snowy Hindu Kush
When the rooftops become pools
Of lapis moon
No one knows this place but me

In daylight the village grows
From lunar fields of pummeled stone
From forty years of war
And as many enemies

In between a river runs through
Which hasn't been fished since seventy-nine
When the Soviets mined
The riverbeds of Afghanistan

Villagers worked inside these walls
Before a bomb in a crowd sent them home
Now I see them in the distance
Ink blots on a gray canvas
Digging in the rubble
Remembering the vineyards and crops
That painted this valley emerald green
When the fishing was good

Now they dream to work in peace
I dream someday I'll come back
Not as a military man
But as a fly fisherman

In a Perfect World There Are No Questions

Weeks of laboring must have seemed preposterous
to the rattlesnakes and wallowing buffalo, the flooding
monsoon rain.

A man and a movie star fell from the sky in a gold-plated
helicopter to inspect their ancient ruins and toy buffalo herd.

A world divided between the new and the old. Why must
everything I love have some age to it? All those dead
heroes, worn out boots, aboriginal loves.

A life carved into big chunks of time like do I wear a
coat or not. As measured by music of the mockingbird
on the traffic light as I walk to work each morning.

Millions are wasted predicting an impossible future.
Everything we are is the past of memory and the tenuous
present. Except for dreams, which if we're lucky will
lay claim on the future.

Quanah's house sighs at night, sucking summer through
broken windows, blowing holes in the roof between giant
white stars fading and falling to the earth.

Sandstone boulder. Mud ripples fossilized in stone. Touching
them I realize my problems are inconsequential in the big
scheme of things.

In a perfect world there are no questions. Nobody cares.
Birds and dogs and a few old Indians know this. Sleep when
sleepy. Eat when the belly trembles. Cry out when it hurts.

When What Is Made to Fuse Together Cannot

She said it's safe to speak
In the language of pottery
Like a body it's a gift

From the soft bottom upward
Across time
And rumors of the smoke shadow face
Of its creator
And the scent of ancient pollen
Entombed in caramel glaze

A delicate neck painted in birds
With the hair from a child
A necklace jeweled
From punched bone

A lip so full
So thirsty
It spills cold water from within
Coil memory skin
Breathing
Cooling
Cracking when fired too hot
When what is made to fuse together cannot

Fallen Bird

how alike are the birds in the olive tree
which live in the symbol of peace
they have no who they are the good birds
which represent amnesty
they have no who they are reality's rumor
they make music and metaphors
for possibility they signal and harbinger
because they sing in the olive tree
and war among themselves and fall
                              —Sharon Jones

Sharon Jones gave me this poem ten years ago. I didn't understand it back then because I'd yet to become a full-fledged bird. I hung it on the wall, hoping that someday I'd understand what she was trying to tell me.

That was a time of simultaneous beauty and pain when life and death weren't so far apart. A time when I learned I was an artist. I covered up the poem with a painting and it became lost to me.

Last year I wanted so much to have the poem, to find it hiding behind the forgotten art. I thought it might have been a dream, the poem and that part of my life. Then, as I was unpacking some things, I had the feeling the poem was near. I took off the backing from of a framed aquarelle and there it was, Sharon's poem, my poem. Typed beautifully, signed in blue, glued to a paper border the color of wet adobe.

Sharon was the real deal. She wrote spontaneously on an old typewriter. She detested titles, revising, capitalization, punctuation. She wrote not to be read, admired or criticized. She wrote to breathe, to live, in the process teaching others to live.

Tonight, a thousand crickets from the patio, the sound of earth buzzing. And the chatter of cottonwood leaves, the ticking of Earth's time. I can hear the moonglow too, its pale vibrations. A deer bounds up the far bank of the creek, popping through a hole between red cedars into the black.

Tonight I have no who. I am a good bird. Sharon was like that too, a songbird in an olive tree, fighting her war so there could be peace.

I learned recently that she died of cancer.

Fallen bird.

Dear Sharon

You published one book in '74.
But then again what really matters
are the hundreds of your beautifully
typed poems tucked away in the
places poetry lives.

Bookmarking a page in *One Hundred
Years of Solitude* on its seventh read.
Pinned to the Frigidaire with a travel
magnet. Concealed behind an
aquarelle in an old picture frame,
waiting for the courage to reappear.

You once wrote that you are more
real than the centuries of space
between a bird's wings. I guess
what I'm trying to say is you are
dead but will never really die.

Slow Burn

They removed from Americans
the ability to sit still.
But I'm here
on the other side of the world,
where every night is a slow burn
of exploding sky
and tobacco painting the stars blue.

I'm here,
removed from their efforts to engineer
spontaneity from the culture.
Their sagging shelves of bric-a-brac,
small talk,
escapisms,
the need to be entertained.

I'm here
wondering if I'm still an American.

Ramadan Moon

"What's that round disk you are lighting, tobacco?"

"Oh my God," said Medina. "Nooooo, this is charcooool! To burn the tobacco in the hookah. It's peach flavored, you know?"

It was peachy, but being an Okie I was slow to the take, causing Medina to ask, "Oh my God, haven't you ever smoked a Hoooookah? Where have you been? Oh my God! You know, you have to suck the thing, like this . . ."

I spoke of birds, that perhaps they are the only creatures not ruined by hominal violence in Afghanistan. But Ariana disagreed, insisting that birds are imprisoned in a mile-long drainage ditch running the length of a nearby street, an iron grate covering the top. When she walks the birds follow along underground, trying to escape, screaming like a Parwan prisoner. I said I thought those were frogs not birds. To think that they may be birds is horrifying.

A couple of jets took off, splitting the full moon with their afterburners, causing the earth to tremble. The terrifying noise woke the mynah birds in a nearby mulberry. Its branches shivered in waves with the flutters of a thousand wings, their horrible squawks sounding like torture.

"Oh my God, I hate those birds, you know? Oh my God! They are always screeching outside my room. Sometimes I open the window and scream SHUUUT UUUP YOU BITCHES, which usually works. Oh my god!"

Medina and Ariana, Pashtuns from Kandahar, by way of the Bronx. They are not the typical long-suffering, terrorized Afghan women. No, they are Afghan Americans, with tattoos peaking from places I love. They know how to curse too, Bronx style. But their eyes are Afghan.

Blue Democracy

There are pomegranate trees and plenty of blue,
cerulean skies,
a mosque painted indigo.

This election's a terminal kismet.
The polling station's open but nobody's there.
The last time around they cast their votes
with fingers dipped in sapphire ink,
as the fading light turned cochineal,
then a dark they'd never seen.

When the villagers awoke
there were no blue fingers anymore.
Severed in the night by shadows black,
heaped in a pile
burning blue
and pomegranate red.

Will the children bloom like Afghan roses
or fly off dead in the shape of question marks?
I can't remember the last time I voted,
but they'll never forget.

New Horizon

A fundamental lesson is to fish without a hook. Catch and release is a compromise, as much pain for the fish as a tattoo but usually survivable, their essence inked into some crease of my memory made of water and nerves beneath bone.

There's a painful silence in the West louder than a sonic boom. No one can hear it before the coming storm. CNN and cereal and sleep are a toxic combination during a government shutdown. It's important to know what we'll wear to the grave as we fear for the children already lost. Everything tastes bad except good whiskey.

A bourbon for lunch seemed necessary after reading of the xenophobic panic that earth's magnetic north is hurtling toward Russia at 34 miles every year.

The bartender mixed a sweet syrup infused with spice and green chile. "Every day there are still firsts! What is this?"

"The world's best breath mint."

Later she caught me pouring whiskey from a flask into my glass while watching golfers on the driving range duff and slice and curse. Even I know that success in golf, like everything else worth doing, is about realizing every swing is an artistic endeavor. Kind of like fishing without a hook.

My new house is a symbol of wilderness encroachment as burrowing creatures undermine the foundation of existence, the ground. My dog has become an amateur archaeologist with her own looted excavations.

Sleeping on the patio I saw a copperhead weaving its way through the grass. I have considerable experience with rattlesnakes but was unprepared for the copperhead, especially its ability to climb rocks and comfortable lawn furniture.

The cottonwoods dance, they come and go, their bones. The footsteps of every ghost to wade this creek since it was a creek, washed away by water the color of old blood. Here now, all at once, like a crowded street corner in Tokyo. Most wearing moccasins and a few leather boots.

I can't keep the squirrels from the bird feeder. I washed the kitchen window at midnight to watch the morning geese fly between the outstretched arms of two cottonwoods, my new horizon. Every day I dream about the Land of Enchantment not realizing it's already here.

1193 Miles

for Heather

Might as well be the distance light travels
from your black star
to my satellite eyes.
Too much distance to fathom
outside poetry.

Tonight,
my satellite is tinny and frail,
barely able to hang above the pull
of this tiny flotsam planet's
blue gravity.

Before morning,
will it burn in the atmosphere
or catch a ride on a miracle wish,
beyond the terrible constraints
of time and space?

Beyond,
that is where love lives.

To Speak Their Names

The Chinese said there were many
gods in the body but to speak their
names was to lose them.

I like to think of all the names we
have for birds and what these tiny
gods may call themselves. Thank
god we'll never know. If we could
speak their names we'd lose them too.

It's sad we don't realize we were small
gods, before we learned to speak
our names ten-thousand times a day.

Happy Endings

He felt his heart flutter from the shock of rotary blades whirling on the tarmac. They seemed to split the air open then out, beyond the speed of sound. Nothing should travel that fast except the cosmos.

The Chinook came in fast, just above the treetops, landing in a soccer field. It was on the ground long enough for him to grab his bag and run. Then it was airborne, up over the tall concrete walls, disappearing into the city.

He made his way to the most heavily guarded swimming pool in the world at the Embassy. On a whim he performed a lopsided cannonball, soaking a big-bellied diplomat wearing a candy-striped speedo.

Later that evening he was late to a business dinner. Finally showing up he said, "Boys, I'm embarrassed to admit I was held up at the massage parlor", provoking a round of wisecracks about happy endings.

At night a transvestite sat across from him at a picnic table. When he complained of the long days she responded, "I've been here six years working twelve-hour days, seven days a week, only going home once at my own expense. I've lived in the same metal box for six years with the same roommate. He's never spoken to me. My life comes down to work and television because I'm afraid of the night. I'd like to travel more but I'm afraid to go alone and have no money." She must have been terrified because it was the middle of the night. He wondered what she was doing there. He thinks he knows.

He went to a blue rooftop café with a view of the moon rising above the perimeter wall. From his perch he could see Afghan boys playing volleyball which they love. There were likeminded people hunched over notebooks, dreaming of whiskey, smoking cigarettes. Somewhere he read that the hysteria over smoking coincided with the decline of communism, no doubt true.

How he enjoyed that blue café perched above the bleeding city, with its eternal heroin wounds. America is high he thought, as Afghanistan bleeds. He wished he was the black cat on his lap, so he could explore the city at night without risk of human violence.

Before leaving, he had a bird's eye view of a suicide bomber blowing himself up outside the nearby airport. His target was a former warlord, returning from exile. But he only managed to kill twenty of his men and a photojournalist.

He flew from the soccer field on a different kind of bird, up over the pines, disappearing. He's back home now not wanting to be.

Who Are You

after Tom Waits

Rilke said everything is gestation
And then bringing forth

I'm your red house wondering why
Until I heard your song again
Lost for a thousand years
Until you fed me blood wine
Now I know who I am
A star reborn from ice

I live in darkness
Where moonglow dances blue
But without night there would be no day
I watch the moon travel to you yesterday
The only time I'll admit

I built a time machine
Not to know which horse won
But to play on your rusty swing set
One more time
As the train flies by
On its way to Albuquerque

Tucumcari

When dreams turn dark the vultures dance
They feed on the eyes of a newborn calf
And pick the highway clean
Making love to rotting flesh

Poor vulture
The only bird without romance
But watch them swoon
In their canopy of blue

Ink black stains on pale sky
Their shadows sweep the desert's dust
Hard to tell a vulture
From a loitering drone

Strip it away
The stringy moist things
The droop and flem
The stench of road kill
There's an ugliness in fear
Vultures don't kill

Black winged wedge of sky
Keeping the Mexican road crew company
And me
Tucumcari

Shadow Dancing

walking westward
in the time of bird migrations
and cool shadows
the sunrise an amber wash of light
against our backs
her shadow touching mine
merging for a moment
and forever
here on this page
shadow dancing

Satellite Television Signal Loss

A cottonwood holds the creek bank.
She's deathly allergic to late spring,
when cottony parachutes fill the nests

of birds and blanket new grass like snow.
She can't understand why I spend so
much time back there. Or my neighbor,

telling me he called the city to have the
tree removed. Something about satellite
television signal loss.

Just Fishing

Out on the Matagorda flats
The fly fishermen stand
Hip deep in green water
Watching the shoal grass grow
Waiting for a single blade twitch
Redfish

Aransas Pass
Where the air is heavy and wet
A quarter mile out
On pink granite boulders
As big as washing machines
Where the waves break far into the bay
And the pelicans hop-fly over them
Fishing the calm between
Then up over white caps to fish again
Working hungry
Hours each day

Out there
The fishermen have no fancy boats
Just a rod and reel
And a dog or two
Fishing
Just fishing

A Love Supreme

Dog's collar, bleached white bones
Icons of yarn and nip and paperback strips
Stuck in the sweetgrass
The Taos sky a windblown gray

Penitente heart, penitente wind
Crying in the cottonwood grove
Disco dance under broken bourbon glass
Trinkets and tin and cellophane
Spinning shards of silver light

High on the mountain her wind sings
As pine bough strings
Strumming
His colorless dreams
Nieves penitentes
Pointing icy fingers to the noonday sun
Solar radio hums
Sangre de Cristo

Old man river far below
Cold and low
Before it sings of spring
A magpie sings to her lover
Undercover willow canopy
Tail above nest
Water steams from a skinny-dipping spring
Singing "A Love Supreme"

Self Portrait

What I read and drink is somewhat limited.
The only source of reliable information is
poetry. I'd love to fall in love with red wine
but can't afford the good stuff.

Birds are tiny gods although I'm no
birdwatcher. I have no interest in cataloguing
or naming except to know what they call
themselves. I have many favorites but they
seem to change a lot. But I'll always love
crows, the way they wait by the highways
like the widows of Juarez and Kabul.

I'd like to become more beautifully indifferent
like trees, although I'm no farmer to love
a piece of earth forever. Before I set
a taproot, the next storm carries me away.
I don't have any close friends within six
hundred miles of home but beyond that, many.

I'll always dream of Paris and Madrid even
though I'm just an Albuquerque kind of guy.
Berlin is out of the question because they were
so awful to the Jews.

Miller Williams said everyone is a battlefield.
I don't trust anyone without a pocketful of
secrets. There is a hole in my pocket but I always
keep it full so I don't have to wear the iron mask
I threw away at forty.

I like the jazz of Chet Baker, the blues of
Lightnin' Hopkins, any cowboy songs
sung by old men.

I like to dream of simple things like waking
up early, writing until noon, cooking dinner,
going to the bar. When I need to recharge the
batteries, getting lost on a highway pointed
anywhere, flying along with birds.

Cante Jondo

sing a deep song
of the death of things before
of coppery mountains hiding
under a blanket of new snow

of the burning Afghan sun
blotted by Kabul smoke

of the hundred women waiting in line
their first would be their last
deep song
a vote

sing a deep song
of the birth of ancient questions
why are we here
why there's no such thing as win

Bird Feet, Feathered Wings

She is common mallow. He is hollyhock. Tall
and brittle in mid-summer, a head above the weeds
near the bus stop. Their secret purple garden,
nourished by the blowing trash of humanity.

She's a friend to everyone who matters and to
one mongrel who does not. All those wandering
spirits. Their faces the burning sun when they'd
see her coming.

She danced across the plaza in heels and fur,
raven hair bucking the blue gravity. He followed
until her scent kissed his nose, rarely certain about
anything in life, except the scent on the collar of
her fur coat. Lilac.

He learned from her that a homeless Navajo boy
with the saddest happy face is as relevant as all
the celebrities huddled around the bar at La Fonda.

Small town near Rainy Mountain where
her ancestors still walk the prairie visiting friends.

She said let your spirit water flow into the acequia
of life, allowing things to grow green where they
shouldn't.

They will always belong to the missed because they
live well. This has nothing to do with economics but
ways of moving in the world with bird feet,
feathered wings.

Broken Empire Heart

He glanced at the capitol rotunda then walked all the way to Adams Morgan, where there was less chance of encountering a trash can bomb or a politician. He looked for a suitable tavern where Merle Haggard was on the jukebox but was unsuccessful.

He wandered into The Russia House because he liked the neon cocktail sign in the window. The bartender said people don't wear cowboy boots in The Russia House. To ease the bartender's qualified mind, he ordered a heaping plate of borscht with red caviar and no fewer than three top-shelf vodka martinis.

He thought about the highway he'd been traveling, broken in places, most of the good things gone. Route 66 from Sapulpa to the western prairie, scratching words in weathered pavement with a bloody fingernail one letter at a time. Six hundred miles to Santa Fe and the rest of his life.

He thought about how flawed he'd become in the world he was part of most of the time. The world of making things happen. The world of impressions. His life a chain of collusions, leaving his soul a black stone. But that his flaws seemed different when he left the world of making things happen to a place where his spirit was boundless like a bird.

Oblivion comes easy in Washington D.C. even in the week before Christmas. He saw a nitwit wearing a Trump hat make a twenty-foot bypass around a wailing woman with no legs. Gravid was her suffering, as thick as the scent of grease beneath the city of hardened subway arteries flowing to the center of a broken empire heart.

Stray Dogs

Ziziphus tree sings of birds.
Crows dance on the horizon.
To dream in the Arabian desert!

Awake,
the tree is dead.
They are not crows
but stray dogs picking
ten-thousand trash piles
at the messy edge of the city.

I used to think the treatment of dogs
and the health of a culture
were congruent.
But in America
the dogs are better fed than the poor,
as it commits suicide
like all the other air-conditioned empires
of history.

Church Tavern

Their church was in a certain bar at night. Then
during the day in a cathedral of shade under the skirt
of a cottonwood out back. Flawed saints, though
not in the modern prefabricated religious sense.

An old man hobbled in with a cane and ordered
a tall double whiskey, the only obvious way to
build courage for the barfly next to him.

A billboard on the highway says LUST IS SINFUL.
Nearby there is a tavern where the women
go topless when George Jones plays on the jukebox.

Fuck the two-hundred-dollar seat on the forty-yard
line. The view is better from the Stonewall Tavern,
sitting next to the sweet profanity that is John.

C.D. is a ninety-four-year-old black man who's
been coming to this redneck bar since 1953.
There's nothing else to say except he's one
tough hombre.

In a bar in Santa Fe I saw an old windblown
cowboy who could be me in twenty years. When
his cell phone rang he answered in perfect French,
"Bonjour mon amour".

No friendly faces in the Lonesome Dove Saloon.
A sign on the door should say NO VACANCY.
Just down the road another sign reads DANGER—ARTILLERY
MAY BE FIRED OVER ROADS IN THIS AREA.

The bartender's grandfather recited Poe from
memory every time they'd meet. The day after he
died her patrons noticed the large raven tattooed
above her breasts.

"Where am I?" asked a trucker who'd been on
the road for three years.
"It's pretty simple. You're in the middle of it all,
but you still have a long way to go."

Hiking from Mexicali to the Sea of Cortez.
Turned back by a hive of pickpockets and youthful
lust, getting no further than a dingy whorehouse bar.

She said something about running out of toilet
paper two weeks ago, improvising with _____.
I didn't hear that part but the mind runs wild
with possibilities.

Linda rescued nine girls from an oilfield
whorehouse in Seminole County. She put them to
work in her tavern on the edge of town, where one
night Conway Twitty fathered the words to a hit song.

In Stillwater they cram for finals at the bar with
beer for breakfast and plenty of cigarettes and
country music.

You know it's going to be good when before noon
you must two-step from the front door to the bar.

Luna

The movement of the past few weeks left him blurry and muted. But clarity came with the help of friends at a no-name bar on the old highway at the edge of town. He couldn't remember what it used to be called, for the sign blew away in a tornado years ago. But then again nobody cared. It wasn't the kind of place that catered to tourists from the nearby Interstate.

Luna had an interest in history, having named her toddler son Tiberius. She also played the flute, and, being a "bad girl", spent plenty of time in juvenile detention growing up. She said one day her dad stumbled into the sometimes strip club after a long day of fishing. When he discovered she was a stripper he was very angry although he later renamed his beloved 1969 Chevelle Luna.

The night before returning to the war he went back to the no-name bar for reasons of nostalgia. It was the last bar he'd see for many months. And also because Luna was supposed to be working. But Cherokee Bill said that her baby daddy put her in the hospital along with their son Tiberius, adding, "After baby daddy gets out of jail I'm going to string him up by the pecker from the disco ball and let the girls have their revenge!" Then Lonnie, a 300-pound Bandido biker, added, "I've got ten heavily wooded acres with plenty of room to hide what's left of baby daddy after the girls finish with him."

There is a sweet spot an hour before closing time when it's best to leave a bar like that or at least lay claim to the barstool nearest the door. The time just before the collective weariness of a week's hard labor in the oil fields is overcome by loneliness, lust and booze paranoia, the perfect ingredients for violent sinning in the parking lot. So, he left before the sinning commenced, although it would have been better to roll the dice at closing time.

He rode home in a double barrel rain squall, dodging windblown branches across the dark highway. There was so much rain his boots filled with water. There was a time or two when he wondered if he'd be joining Luna and Tiberius in the hospital that night.

Oso Grill

Fried pickles and catch of the day,
cheap canned beer.
Wind blowing spring storms from the Gulf.
Eight hours fly fishing the Laguna Madre
without a redfish.

A fisherman says,
every year thousands of butterflies
stop to rest on his shrimp boat
on their long journey home
before they die.

A dolphin rolls off the lip of a turquoise wave
in Corpus Christi Bay.
A pretty picture,
even with the spew of refineries in the distance.

The wind just blew my beer can off the table,
so it's time for another.
This place,
beautifully flawed like me.

Chicken Factory

Boredom can be dangerous in youth, chasing
madcap dreams as easy as driving a hundred
miles an hour on a dirt road at midnight. Turn
the lights off to see if anyone's coming, then
blow through the stop sign.

Like the time my cousin and I dreamed of buying
motorcycles to ride to Florida for the rest of our
lives. It would be easy after all to get a job at
the chicken factory on a bank of the Arkansas
River next to the county jail. Save a little money.

They issued head-to-toe rubber impedimenta to
clean the stink and guts off stainless steel surfaces
on the night shift. It was summertime but cold,
cold chemical splatter sweats. Shoveled out rolling
bins of unfit chicken parts bound for the dogfood factory.

During the day we slept in my Grandmother's
iron bed with sagging springs. A box fan in
the window pointed at our heads, wet hair
blowing asleep.

It only took three nights to get sick from the chemicals
in that industrial nightmare and the sharpening
sense of fear working alongside hardened men with
face tattoos, addicts, ex-prisoners and a jailbreak or
two. It only took three nights to unrealize our dream.

My grandmother cut two straws. My cousin
picked the long one which meant the Marine Corps.
That's how I joined the Navy, growing up very fast,
learning how to dream the right way.

Common Swift

I saw a few of your scouts as you were making
your way from Africa. I thought you were cliff
swallows or purple martins. But no, you are swifts,
with sickle wings and forked tails.

This morning was like stepping into the lorikeet
cage at the Oklahoma City Zoo as hundreds of
you flittered about. Your wings nearly touched
my ears like whispers of the gods.

You hold the record for the longest bird flight,
living in the air for ten months, coming here
to build nests on the south side of an abandoned
Soviet hangar where it's warm and protected.

Do me a favor, stay in the air, or at least up on a
wire. You are stumbling drunkards on the earth,
without fear but easy pray for careless soldiers' boots.

I thought I heard Bruce Springsteen, but it was you
singing baby we were born to fly, because you are
undoubtedly part of the sky.

Mexicali Song

Chorus:
Well it's twenty years later, but it seems like yesterday
I hope you made it out of Mexicali OK

Ain't it funny how dreams just appear
Maybe not so funny, you're somewhere and I am here
Don't get me wrong, I've had a good life
A job with good pay, A lovely daughter and wife

Remember when I asked if you'd run with me tonight
Get out of this whorehouse, across the borderline
You smiled for a moment and my heart skipped a beat
But then your eyes teared up as you stepped to the street

Searchin' for meaning in a world full of blues
Can't read the morning paper, can't watch the evenin' news
No use payin' attention or stickin' around
When I dream of your smile, I was lost but now I'm found

Bird Symphony

There was the dream of walking the streets of the City of Angels once again in boots. Also eating a steak dinner in a red leather booth with a fancy cocktail at Jack's. Then wandering over to lose his mind at the Viper Room, where he saw her father's band play so long ago. She was on tour with the band instead of in school, keeping watch over him, even though she was only thirteen. He imagined her in front of a cracked mirror in the dressing room, smoking cigarettes, pretending to be the rock star she would become years later to him and the world.

But he was a long way from Los Angeles as he sat there on a picnic table reading *The Paris Review,* choking down a questionable chow hall dinner of chicken nuggets and soda pop. Remembering the color when he thought the Afghan spring would never end. But now he was consumed by the hard-boiled summer, staring at what was left of the brittle leaves and a brown dust halo on the horizon, smudging away the mountain's snowy beacon.

He worried about fading memories of her until she said, "Memories fade into colors and melt into songs." He could hear the sound of her voice as the music of wind through Ponderosa pines near Battleship Rock. He remembered her song, word for word, as vivid in his mind as the crimson sucking chest wound of a soldier the previous week.

It hadn't rained for months, so he craved the scents of spring, especially new rain. He once thought it the best smell in the world until he sniffed his daughter's head when she was three. Wheat and honey. Now older her head still smelled wonderful although different.

Birds vanished. So strange to hear a just a single cicada scout in a locust tree, the blossoms of which smelled as good as lilac in the spring. But the dangling white locust blossoms were long gone, leaving behind brittle seed pods hanging on for dear life. Or would that be death?

Getting up to leave he saw a dead bat on the sidewalk. This made him think about birds not bats. How the birds seemed to have vanished in the mid-summer heat and dust. How he never saw dead birds back home.

He said a little prayer for the birds to return to him in dreams. Who else could he ask what to do? They always seem to know where to go. Remembering how the combined sound of every bird on earth singing used to wake him up at night. God's symphony.

Irina

Twelve hours a day,
seven days a week.
Restorer of worn out pelts.
Standing in puddles of drool
and tears not her own.
But she goes home for a month each Christmas.
"I assume they pay your way?"
"No, that's why I need a big tip from you."

Lost Suitcase

An expert on television suggested the base of a temple could
not have been built by the Phoenicians and was therefore a
landing pad for alien spacecraft. Archaeology has become the
archaeology of aliens, as people of antiquity were evidently too
stupid to understand the cosmos or build elaborate temples. I find
it much more interesting to note that Christopher Columbus had
to rely on the navigation of birds and the indigenous people he
would soon enslave followed the stars.

I no longer care about spectacular ruins, just tiny historical
conundrums. Like the story about the Spanish poet Antonio
Machado abandoning a suitcase full of unpublished poems,
as he fled from Franco's fascists to Paris. He insisted on being
the last to board an ambulance truck bound for the French
seaside village of Collioure. When he saw there was no more
room, he picked up his ailing mother and boarded the truck
without the suitcase.

Machado never made it to Paris because he died at Collioure,
staring at the sea. He drowned not from it but pneumonic fluid.
Instead of alien landing pads television should air documentaries
about the search for Machado's suitcase, surely one of the most
significant lost treasures in the world.

The Barber

She wore rings with fire agate
and turquoise to see the sunrise
and blue sky on cloudy days.
She kept a fossil in her pocket
to ballast daily problems,
insignificant within the sweep
of geology's time.

I said I came to Tulsa to pay
respects to Yevtushenko and to
whisper thanks from a friend
for his poem "Babi Yar" about
Nazi atrocities committed upon
the Jews of Kiev.

"You know, he once sat right
there in his colorful sweater,
watching me cut hair for hours,
finally saying, your scissors are
a painter's brush. You are an artist."

Butterfly Storm

the silence between
seasons on the prairie
when the wind stands still
for no more than a few hours
between great shifts
when everything waits
for something to happen
just enough time
for a congregation of monarchs
to confuse the weatherman
with a butterfly storm
before the wind blows cold
pushing them all the way to Mexico

Cliff Dwelling Near Bluff Utah

They were young, digging between the
bones of ancestors not their own. Bathing
in powder sugar dust that never mixed with
rain. As rain, washing away the conquest
of Anglo time.

Digging in the name of science, but really
because they were hollowed out, searching
for human ways of moving in the world.

So they dug a hole, leaving their watches
there, and have been late for everything
that's supposed to matter ever since.

Afghanistan Suite

My wings are broken I can't move. Waiting for the
moon if there is a moon in this world of disappearing.

Maybe the only ones not ruined by hominal butchery
are migratory birds.

Are birds the same just with different names? Unbearable
the life without mockingbird, meadowlark, crow.

Looking up I saw a giant holding the patio umbrella a
hundred feet in the sky. Letting go, a red kite over Kabul
before we ruined the place.

I pretend to have abundant courage. But bleeding
Afghanistan with no wine to temper the madness beneath
kite-less skies?

O Bordeaux, nectar'd bees and butterflies! These
agricultural thoughts will get me arrested. I should have
stocked the mental cupboard in advance of the ensuing
draught.

***

Everything is lawless including sleep. My afterburner
dreams.

If this is not another planet then it's the far side of the
moon. Lunar cold and dark, without an atmosphere.

An explosion. Then the unholy sound of air expelled
from the depths of my lungs, burning upwards into
embarrassment. The sound of death before dying.

With trickery and guns they pinned us into a house at the end of a street. They found me staring out the back window at an eagle high in a pine tree above a frozen stubble field.

Desert lips deprived. Vague tummy rumblings. A sign over the sink reads sanitized unpotable water.

Gray gravelly everything except a stand of Russian thistle flashing purple eyelashes next to tumbleweeds that don't tumble across the highway like they do in west Texas.

***

Her scent loiters in the desert sans competition. Vivid as violet on a white palette. Red mingling with true blue. No mere evocation but a double barrel bouquet. A lingering, chromatic sillage.

To glance into her eyes held such consequence. The beauty of the world painted on a tiny canvas of green eyes, black mascara, framed by a veil coal black.

Reading Anais Nin's diary in a café full of women wearing burkas. What would Henry Miller think?

Bedouins wander as white ghosts across the effervescent Desert. Beneath hives of power lines and refinery spew, clusters of white tents, camels in the courtyard. Parked out front, Cadillacs.

"Bedouin hipster?" I asked a man wearing a long robe, sandals and a trucker's cap.
"How can you tell?" he asked.

***

A dove not a hawk. I hate guns but can shoot the tits off a boar at thirty yards.

Who can say they've walked four miles in frozen darkness to buy toothpaste? Who can say they don't remember except for the cyclopean red moon hanging above the pines?

Reading alone. The others small talking about the day, when we were killed with rubber bullets in the hostile cold. One of them asking, "What's wrong?" Looking down I said, "Poetry."

***

Apple cheek on apricot wrist
Lipstick, pistol on her hip
Machine gun slung
Sleeping

O My
Time speeds by
Pen out of ink
I can't think

Ooo eeee
Strange body whiff
The Taliban blew up the PX
Thank god for Amazon.com

Picnic table, morning tree
Cigarettes, black coffee
Pakistani laborers sweeping the dust
Happy lonely heart broke

Tending the roses
Friday mornings
Bird shit on my head
I don't care

Lonely prickly pear
With only one pad
Coffee grounds in the garden
Trying to grow more

Bark of the locust
Old man skin
Tears form then fall
Strange times of the day

Bought a pack of smokes
To remember the glimmer
Of her face that night
Red rose ember

Birds are dying
In this dying place
But there are plenty more
To send her way

Walk in the morning
Walk at night
Duct tape covers
A hole in my boot

The days are so long
But nights are without time
Pájaro hermoso
I'm doing just fine

***

Azimi said the crude painting was of his father
and grandfather, before the Taliban captured their
village, killing them both. Obviously the most significant
painting in the world.

Cinderblock sinks a liquid heart. Eyes full of rain.
Doing things slowly. Taking what I can get. Permitir más
recuerdos.

O Afghanistan. How much is left of your broken heart?
A heart that once knew the ways of what was to be
done before the madness of the world? Interminable
bleed without a tourniquet.

An Afghan rose pushes the sky one last time, burdened
by water.

A Russian pocket watch keeps no time. Just to remember
This place by. The vulgarity of clocks, burden of drifting
time, heavy as water.

***

Over yonder in Kabul skeletons creeps to the radio tower.
Dreadful draught. Refugees returned with nothing on
their backs but sacks of adobe bricks. Someday the
rain's gonna fall, washing them all back down. Bricks,
bones, riverbed clog.

They speak our language but we can't speak theirs. They
sound so different but they all look the same. Disposable
clothes. American hoodie hegemony.

Afghan boys stacking sandbags all day. Ugandan guards,
Kalashnikovs slung like gunmetal guitars. The insider
threat is real.

Sun shining, nose rosy red. This tobacco cowboy's rough
as the lizard boots he's wearing.

***

My favorite days are the in-betweens, forgotten by
the economy and history. Thanksgiving's come and
gone. It should be my favorite holiday, but like attending
mass it comes with a sense of irony. Christmas too but
not this year. Christmas bourbon, sleeping bag on the patio,
sparrows in the snow. O, I'll never forget to hang the
lights again!

Every evening a pinch of Afghan dust to the wind. Looking
down at all the layers between. Pretty soon all I'll have
to do is look to the west as the sun sets. That's where
she'll be.

On a high desert plain framed by blue mountains, a
beginning. This is the end, I'm leaving.

About the Author

Christopher Brooks lives and works in Saudi Arabia. His educational background is in the archaeology of the southwestern United States. He is a Navy veteran and works in civil service, where he has served in the Pacific Rim, Afghanistan, and the Middle East. His first collection of poems, *With Them I Move,* was published by Finishing Line Press in 2018. His poetry has also appeared in numerous journals, including *Hiram Poetry Review, Flint Hills Review, Dragon Poet Review, Blue Collar Review, Slant: A Journal of Poetry, Red Earth Review, Fly Fishing and Tying Journal,* and the Woody Guthrie Poets anthology *Ain't Gonna Be Treated This Way* (Village Books Press, 2017).

www.ingramcontent.com/pod-product-compliance
Lightning Source LLC
Chambersburg PA
CBHW071357090426
42738CB00012B/3146